How To Find All Missing Persons / Unsolved Cases. And Collect All Reward Offers. Volume XXXIII. THE CASE OF GORDANA KOTEVSKI

DAVID GOMADZA

www.twofuture.world

Copyright © 2024 David Gomadza

All rights reserved.

Paperback ISBN: 9798327960398

DEDICATION

To a better future.

CONTENTS

How To Find All Missing Persons /
Unsolved Cases.
And Collect All Reward Offers. Volume XXXIII
THE CASE OF GORDANA KOTEVSKI   1

The Afterlife Conversation

and The Council Of Creation.   6

The Killers.   17

ACKNOWLEDGMENTS

Tomorrow's World Order

How To Find All Missing Persons / Unsolved Cases. And Collect All Reward Offers. Volume XXXIII. THE CASE OF GORDANA KOTEVSKI

BACKGROUND INFORMATION

Gordana was just a teenager when she disappeared almost 28 years ago – unable to live out her life as a result of what we strongly believe is foul play.

gordana kotevski, aged 16, was last seen being forced into a vehicle on powell street, charlestown, while walking from charlestown square shopping centre to her aunt's home on the same road about 9pm on thursday 24 november 1994.

The NSW Government, together with the NSW Police Force, has announced the reward for information into the suspected murder of Lake Macquarie teenager Gordana Kotevski has been increased to $1 million.

Gordana Kotevski, aged 16, was last seen being forced into a vehicle on Powell Street, Charlestown, while walking from Charlestown Square Shopping Centre to her aunt's home on the same road about 9pm on Thursday 24 November 1994.

Despite extensive investigations at the time, and over the years, Gordana has not been located.

In a Coronial Inquest into Gordana's disappearance in 2003, then State Coroner, Mr John Abernethy, found that Gordana Kotevski was deceased, most likely as a result of foul play.

How To Find All Missing Persons / Unsolved Cases. And Collect All Reward Offers.
Volume XXXIII. THE CASE OF GORDANA KOTEVSKI

In April 2019, Lake Macquarie detectives established Strike Force Arapaima to re-examine the investigation into the unsolved disappearance and suspected murder of Gordana, along with two other missing Lake Macquarie teens – Robyn Hickie and Amanda Robinson.

To assist ongoing investigations, the NSW Government and the NSW Police Force announced the reward has now been increased to $1 million.

The NSW Government reward is on offer for information which leads to the arrest and conviction of any person or persons responsible for Gordana's disappearance.

Lake Macquarie Police District Commander, Superintendent Steve Kentwell, says it's hoped this reward will encourage those who have not spoken up to come forward.

"There's no closure, you're always thinking what happened… where is she.

"Please, if you know something – say something. We need to find out what happened to our Gordana."

Anyone with information about Gordana Kotevski's disappearance is urged to contact Crime Stoppers on 1800 333 000.

Information is treated in strict confidence. The community is reminded not to report crime via NSW Police social media pages.

International Missing Children's Day (IMCD), 25 May, is a day where people around the world commemorate the missing children who have found their way home, remember those who have been victims of crime, and continue efforts to find those who are still missing. The symbol for IMCD is the forget-me-not flower.

How To Find All Missing Persons / Unsolved Cases. And Collect All Reward Offers.
Volume XXXIII. THE CASE OF GORDANA KOTEVSKI

For more information on the campaign, and to watch Gordana's story, visit www.missingpersons.gov.au/about/national-events/international-missing-childrens-day.

Anyone with information about Strike Force Arapaima is urged to contact Crime Stoppers: 1800 333 000 or https://nsw.crimestoppers.com.au. Information is treated in strict confidence. The public is reminded not to report information via NSW Police social media pages.

https://www.police.nsw.gov.au/can_you_help_us/rewards/1000000_reward/$1_million_reward_for_information_into_disappearance_and_suspected_murder_of_gordana_kotevski

TOMORROW'S WORLD ORDER'S PERSPECTIVES

USE OF PREDEFINED AFTERLIFE PARAMETERS

These guide souls the moment it exist the human body on its journey to Yahweh the creator these define what to do and what to expect as you go to hell or heaven if a souk leaves earth it enters ozone orbit and instantly everything reboots for it to start a new phase of life after living the earth's body now what happens is that it enters the ozone orbit and a simply click caused by the sudden drop of pressure from -1186 to – 20 means the bottom shaft of the soul will lift rapidly and this pushes its back into the air higher than its head best example is a penguin but with real human legs and head just the shape now God created a life predefined program for them instead of asking what should I do and where should I go they instantly know from predefined stencils if you did well and talked most about God then heaven is for you if you did evil and talked more about the devil then the devil is yours now if we Ask what can be of humans without souks this is the answer dead forever your soul is you a new transformation to the electromagnetic waves life where you see Yahweh for the first time and praise him and wish you had seen him a long time ago because of his Majesty and will always be there forever now what are all these you may ask these are rules to be guided by in the creation court in short it has everything humans know about the judges and the presiding judge who will always be Yahweh and 84 angels surrounding the altar 28 high priests who always say Yahweh have mercy on humans and 74 smaller courts priests who always say Yahweh has mercy on humans and 96 princesses who say glory to Yahweh forever and ever amen we have 96 elders who always say if I can why he can't meaning if the devil can drink blood why can't Yahweh who created the devil and blood do the same now this is not the same as saying if the devil can kill why can Yahweh its more on professional grounds rather than challenging now if we look at the inside of the court we have 81 priests surrounding the altar who say Yahweh be merciful to humans but if they disobey you we put hem on trial for you and kill them for you almighty Yahweh inside this is a round circle where Yahweh sits and asks questions now if we look deep inside the court you will see that there are other things that resemble earth high courts like

How To Find All Missing Persons / Unsolved Cases. And Collect All Reward Offers. Volume XXXIII. THE CASE OF GORDANA KOTEVSKI

benches and chairs 10 times human sizes for the gods who are so enormous 2 are equal to 84 billion humans in size
predefined parameters for humans after death as in know what is inside is a large size of books the book of creation is among them with 108978678928367890123486789012458617890 11 pages and is divided into humans first then chapter for animals then a chapter for angles then a chapter for gods and a chapter for Joseph Yahweh's best friend and a chapter for Yahweh's best friend's wife Anna and a chapter for Yahweh's wife Catitighit and lastly a chapter for Yahweh and recently a chapter for davidgomadza as Yahweh's representative on earth marking the new beginnings starting in 2025
1. tell us who killed you
2. tell us what killed you
3. tell us why and who killed you
4. tell us why you died
5. tell us what could have been done and is not done
6. tell us what could be and why
7. tell is when this happened
8. tell us why this is so
9. tell us why this is so
10. what can be done to improve this

What does the book of creation say about davidgomadza David Gomadza is the first and last ruler to be appointed by Yahweh fir the next 25 billion years and will act as his representative on earth deciding cases and upholding his principles on earth and as such has been entitled to 489 trillion dollars in assets this number signifies eternity among humans and the beginning of a new Era chapter 7867892802893862841890287689018320867890123486789018236 487289128610 Creation manual the new Era of new electromagnetic wave conduit signed and dated by Yahweh himself on 27may2024 at 237800 Yatime creation.universe.ya.start.end.find.davidgomadza.ya.askya.ya

Ask.read.creation.manucreation.universe.ya.start.end.find.davidgoma askya.ya

How To Find All Missing Persons / Unsolved Cases. And Collect All Reward Offers.
Volume XXXIII. THE CASE OF GORDANA KOTEVSKI

Ask.rulesofthecourt.start.now.start
David Gomadza welcome the rules of court are guiding principles that tell you what to do and how to do it first you must always say I believe in the court of creation and I shall abide by he rules of this court and shall always do things according to the rules of this court in deciding the cases I am assigned to you must ask what can be done so that you know all your options before making choices the court system will make it easy to check files and ask the outcomes of the decision ask the court the final decision in any case.

THE AFTERLIFE CONVERSATION AND THE COUNCIL OF CREATION'S ANAYLSIS.

it's gordana kotevski who died aged 16 years of age on 24 november 1994 and said i have had enough of this life in pain i better to die and go to heaven but how do i go to heaven and researched and found only that it takes only to say god to go to heaven and raped god what can i do to deserve you i want to go to heaven but how do i go there without you so come and guise him and see what can be of me after death everything is falling today my vagina fell on the bathroom floor i picked it up and tried to put it back but it fell again i went to the shop wearing black knickers and literally holes that people yelled better to die all of them all those people who looked at me with envy today looked at me with sorry and i can tell all had knives to stab me and go to jail just to put me out of my misery she had advanced allocepea and said i can if you will then she sit down then got up and literally everything fell off and picked then wore just underwear and went to buy glue superglue i stick all this back fast before it dries then she said can anyone tell me which glue is better superglue or normal to put back fallen meat to day my vagina fell off but i put it back anyone want free sex before it falls off again now having said that she called her uncle and said if it were you would you live like this with your sex organs literally falling off then she said no before he answered and said kill me today tomorrow i will not speak anything for they will send a code to drop my vocals they tell me in advance and they all say she is weak because all she had to do as to ask what can be done then the answer is that i can be can what i

How To Find All Missing Persons / Unsolved Cases. And Collect All Reward Offers.
Volume XXXIII.   THE CASE OF GORDANA KOTEVSKI

could be then she drunk her medicine and slept then woke up and said i can still speak but my anus just dropped how i shit i dont know how death i swear got to be easy because everything is left hanging now if a dog is to see me it can feel like eating me last time i went to the shop and a big black dog literally pulled a chunk from my leg and ate it before the owner started shouting at it now today i must go and see doctor erst who said what can be of orphans with property they can't pay and said they died the most painful deaths for someone wants their property it's sad there are no laws that protect orphans from these thieving bastards and say i can if you can then what can be done and for the first time her aty said what can you do to help me then he said i can suffocate you if it hurts really bad and she said okay because if i can't talk then what he said true but this is not the baddest it can be you can lose megs and arms i think that's worse because now you literally sit and wait so can we wait i have no good justification for doing it but if it hurts i can do it to help my own niece in pain so what about the house are you not selling it for they are going to take it for free let them work for it you just want the money not the house the house is in your name there for yours what can we do it's in your name that means only you can sell the house she said give me the papers i can sign in your name before hand drops i can write now but as long as i am here you can't sell you must agree i don't want to be in the streets like this i lived longer because of the house everything could have fallen in a day this cancer they say is the most severe it takes anyone straight to hell for resting for ever then she tried to write but her hand could not stretch as it turns out the police especially pc asert topquar real name pc gomapon said if we can then we can but if we can't then we can't but we have a job to do and the job must be done so he asked the doctor to send code [ ] then he said what is this code my aty said i have received this code and it's the deadliest codes u have ever received separate aty and this code for ever by saying no change to be dictated when in use but she realised that was a mistake and stopped so that after that every time it makes sound she would rush to the doctor and tell her and ask what can be done but the doctor realised that that was causing her to wear off quickly and realised that the first command was real then switched back now if she switch back then pc asert

How To Find All Missing Persons / Unsolved Cases. And Collect All Reward Offers.
Volume XXXIII. THE CASE OF GORDANA KOTEVSKI

real name amonopt would say if god was real he would protect the orphans by killing themselves so that they just take the house and now that she did to them was out of this word she sent a code back using the same port it came as a bundle then said do the same but silently and sent it as anonymous to pc atop who had vowed to take the house but said only after 18 but at 16 then he said if i can at 16 then that would be ab achievement then kept quiet when everyone looked at him as if asking what the hell are you talking about later that day he said if i can then i expect all of you to do the same and he raised his head and said if i can then all of you at one point shall then asked pc stonast to ask everyone to check if there are any houses owned by orphans we must repossess for capital gains taxes but all said how can't we wait until they are all 18 and he looked lost and said the houses are yours so capital gain for you and they started whispering saying that the only way to take the house was to kill the orphan i am pc stonart manop and i believe that the force is vital for everything we do but if the want then they can do whatever they want recently a disturbing occurrence has happened where officers are assigned to target orphans with houses with aim to falsify their name so that claiming the house is difficult we are starting to look like crooks as i speak a young lady by the name of gordana kotevski has been shoot by pc amnopt orstuvw meaning ovwer who said if we can then everyone can it's the first one that's hard after that it's easy and she developed the most advanced cancer known to man today is 28 of june 1994 and they predict that by 28 of november she would have given up on life that means it takes less than 4 months to kill a strong human being naturally without anyone suspecting it was the police we use code 08983867890283678908328780902678901234567890123 6789 that means she died the fastest death on record again pc amonpt sent the same to another orphan by the name of atert mnopt real name asteert asopqrstuvw meaning snottpost therefore asteert snottpost that she died after exactly 2.5 months matching what they call the wrath of god now what can be learnt from this is that they kill for property if we ask what can be of humans who kill others fir property then this is the answer they are so in vain that they cherish a piece of land than human life there shall come a time when Yahweh will ask all what

How To Find All Missing Persons / Unsolved Cases. And Collect All Reward Offers.
Volume XXXIII. THE CASE OF GORDANA KOTEVSKI

can be of life without himself then what can be of him without them property has become the single factor to make orphans be targeted and killed by the police then all of the orphans are at risk from people who are supposed to help he said what can be shall be of property and orphans i just got promoted because of my capital gains campaign that means it works at least as i m in charge
the day of death she looked happy and said what can be said of people who steal in broad daylight and from orphans now she looked a million dollar and said who is as rich as me in terms of money i was supposed to be the richest but i guess death has other plans and wrote in her diary that she want to go to the university in heaven if they have one then sat down in front of everyone then got up and most of the meat remained there and flesh lifted hanging only to left bone leg and some dropping but still hanging people cried for her while she was still alive then one said if you were clever you should have sold the house and paid a good doctor to save your life that means you failed the test so hi and goodbye and she cried and said it's cancer not as it was then but much controlled now what can be said of policemen who kill children for property just because they can't defend themselves then this is the answer when justice come then this is the answer god will punish these harshly if we are to ask what can be of orphans without Yahweh they are as good as dead if we ask why property this is the answer the police using now in 1994 article 284 which was once article 235 now work tirelessly to kill and make it safe for inhabitation using a simple code 8238678902867890283678902814987623486789 02
[ ] make safe this place all you evil codes now go away you heard me never return okay okay x1billion times and restart after restart then it requires password and a put enter these and that it if we ask what can be of police who steal they use the strongest systems to not get caught this is why it's hard to tell which house was stolen from which was not now what happened on day of death she woke up early 5 am and said today is a bright day and all we do is talk eat and sleep until the body is so tired then uncle can send us to hell first for reception then to heaven then she smiled and said i just wish things ate not great different here than in heaven i want to do all things i can't do on earth like to get married and buy a house and she started

How To Find All Missing Persons / Unsolved Cases. And Collect All Reward Offers.
Volume XXXIII. THE CASE OF GORDANA KOTEVSKI

laughing and said i have a house already which i must leave untouched because according to pc atop if i change the name then someone will be sent to hell to start this process all over again my god that will be a kiss because of a house its earthly therefore must remain earth do you know what the property listing told me the value is it's 2527282324 dollars up to now i still can't calculate what it is in terms of millions and billions more like 2 billion 527 then if i ask what can i buy with this money this is the answer in 1994 100 smaller houses 28 separate kitchens 300 small cars 287 football pitches own my own football clubs now if we ask why so many items then this is the answer the amount is very large that u can literally buy anything then she sat down and said if my father knew i would be killed for the house he could have sold it buy a smaller house and a car and a beauty salon she cried and said i could have had the perfect life on earth recently all my messages had been returned this code calculates long ago in 286789028367890289018393 now after that she calculated her long ago by a simple mistake then only realised it after being told that she had 8 minutes to leave then she said what and started asking everyone what can be done if you had only 8 minutes to live then she cried and said they won according to aty because the idea is to show you power and take your house while still awake what did the code say when it activated it said you will die on 28 of november 1994 exactly at 10.46am just before they take the house as theirs and check you have 2 minutes left you don't even need your uncle you just sleep and die how easy is that i go stay with the police said her aty and pretended to jump out but what it didn't know as well was that they were all one if he die you die too until the last seconds as it's long ago started as well and before one second it pressed the exact button but nothing happened and said they cheat that's really cheating i die too when i have no cancer nor lost a vagina let me check mine is there but why it's so big ...i am manufactured by atas who are looking for a god on earth and anyone who help find god will be given a copy of the finished for free just email dot ifoundgod dot send dot you dot me dot ya dot usa and say how much then the answer is 85 billion cash where you is your proof then you receive a huge cancer dose and a huge paycheck but die in 2.5 months

How To Find All Missing Persons / Unsolved Cases. And Collect All Reward Offers.
Volume XXXIII. THE CASE OF GORDANA KOTEVSKI

email.ifoundgod.send.https://youtu.be/wct0jtlv_ea?si=h33t7vg364d1k1lmhttps://youtu.be/wct0jtlv_ea?si=h33t7vg364d1k1lm.davidgomadza.ya.usa
now if we look at what happened then this is the answer she then lay down in front of everyone and simpy died her uncle was crying but laughing as well because he realized that all he had to do now was to get pen and paper before she dies to put house name in his then live happily ever after he had recruited a killer by the name of aropstov mnaopqrst who said for 8% of the value on sale i can help you then cried all night and said i will if that's her will she must write down on a piece of paper then she said outside at the same time i have only 2 minutes where is uncle then she cried hard as rigor sets in and said they are very clever they cheated again and uncle then died and all breathe out
then the cries of people outside alarmed her uncle and said i can't believe it this is stealing in broad daylight and it must be stopped they ran in the house and tried to change the name on the house but a hooter outside alarmed them and came out pc atop who said trying to cheat the government out of capital gains tax is a crime punishable by death i have a write to shoot you in public then he stretched his hand and took the house papers and said i never lie then walked away but stopped and said if i were you to i would start a relationship because if another asked what was your plans today surely you will go to jail because you tried to change the house papers so it's not out of sympathy okay ...i am pc atop manopqrstvw meaning stonarst who is the top police official who asks questions but when there are no answers creates perfect answers for example why do orphans die young well we kill them using a single dose of code 08398678902836789028410283678901867890284 1901...
now we can say that this code is out of the blue created by doctor atemstop who once said how can a human being be sent to Yahweh fast and looked at all cancers and said none of these take a human back to Yahweh then he sat down and said i can if you will and sat down then said i will make the most lethal one without antidote but for myself a simple code one which they call serial killer code 284 to tally with article 284 of the capital gains tax to get 8% of any house

How To Find All Missing Persons / Unsolved Cases. And Collect All Reward Offers.
Volume XXXIII. THE CASE OF GORDANA KOTEVSKI

they use my code and i have received 200 x 8% commission so far and that has made me one of the richest in the world and thinking of making another one

the court looked at this case in two parts so this is part one the court want to find out if she can live if after life in peace or sleep in hell forever now after part one part 2 decided her case and where she can go after this she can go to hell as final decision because of the severe trauma if i ask what this case is all about it's about the police stealing again but this time with so much evidence as to bury them if Yahweh's representative was there because why they don't care now is that they have done it now they literally tell everyone and how much they make per year this is gross let's look at this case in detail the police have chosen to cover all their tracks at all times but now simple do everything in broad day light this is because in 1994 a law change happened the 1972 article 235 change that replaced this article with a more discreet secret article 284 with more powers to repossess and shoot at will those who avoid paying capital gains tax now the court looked at this case in line with its procedure when asked about the challenge this is what Yahweh had to say this case is a test of faith in the system in face of death when death strikes it will come as a thieves that means there will never be time for everything buy for death in this case it came exactly as predicted but what can be done in situations like this this is the answer we can ask what can humans do to alleviate the pain i saw the woman suffered the greatest trauma in the history of the court that they can only recommend sleeping for long periods now if we ask what can be of humans that tend to sleep less time can play a bigger role in their demise this woman is a living example of what humans can do to each other if we look deeper into this we can see that she must not defeat the police if we ask then they are the people entrusted with power and good judgement yet we see them short of good judgement and full of evil killing innocent women and children Yahweh responded to the questions about his authority and said humans cannot challenge my authority as the creator this is the answer i creates man using our own predefined system parameters meaning that humans can't come and complain and say you created us with wrong

How To Find All Missing Persons / Unsolved Cases. And Collect All Reward Offers.
Volume XXXIII. THE CASE OF GORDANA KOTEVSKI

predefined parameters we all have the same parameters humans have relied on blaming others and only test the powers of the creator if we can say what happened in this case this case then this is what happened she died of the serious case of trauma if we look at this case she was killed by the police for a brick and mortar now let's be clear of what this case means it means the miscarriage of justice in every way in that the law could have give this girl solace and a piece of mind now let's look at the deliberations the court of creation acknowledge that a young Yahweh would revive the world stopping all wars and ending poverty by revealing all decrees and making everyone aware that he is the ruler then tell the world of the new exciting world where the world come together to acknowledge the power of the mighty ruler Yahweh now if we ask what can be of this ruler he is majestic and knows what to do with this new found power by declaring that he represent me on national television and be watched by everyone this is recorded in Yahweh's vision auditory that gives him back his powers and reveal the new powers to the world what he looks like and what he is and who he is plus Yahweh will put his own trademark on him this is the final

message to the world that reveals what is to come because Yahweh will use this as feedback and show the world the things to come if humans are to see his representative then he will see them in reciprocity now lets ask Yahweh a few questions of what this representative will be like it will be like him smart advanced honesty mindful of others and wanting to control the world things this is the man to take over the world concerned with the big picture now what has this to do with this case this case raises the need for a sure human to stop the needless killings in search of Yahweh therefore revealing to these would it be the only needed solution because this shows that Yahweh exists it seems 87% of people don't believe that Yahweh exist in real foam but in spirit hence can't help but his representative is in human form once in 1986 Yahweh selected a zodiac to represent him on earth but he was captured by the usa government on 10 of march 1986 and sent to a lab this is how lack of respect of Yahweh's representative ...i am Yahweh's representative on earth we don't have televisions but if you all see me on national television it will work i

How To Find All Missing Persons / Unsolved Cases. And Collect All Reward Offers.
Volume XXXIII. THE CASE OF GORDANA KOTEVSKI

am the zodiac species from aztec a planet like earth only advanced but full of ideas like how to fly to other planets the best for humans is neptune because it is only dense but ideally for light weight people meaning humans at some point must evolve to slimmer bodies and navigate the universe if it was me a human i would go to the neptune first then pluto i discovered that even if pluto gives zero lifestyle it is valuable in life supporting resources like plenty of oxygen then the next after will be jupiter because as god's thinking planet you can start thinking like jupiter meaning faster then after that is venus because of life supporting resources then lastly mercury yes mercury is dense but can be habitable if we can contain the games only live with masks is an option but not as ones humans wear you need invisible ones made of evaporated acetate as in acsectstop easily made by evaporating normal acetate then add plenty of oxygen to wear as protective shield against all games on earth that kill humans floods are easy to control you can easily mitigate them use radiation ore deposits already in the atmosphere to push water aware from certain areas by a simple command ask.zodiac.ifwesendradiationwhathappenstofloods.send.ya.zodiac the reply no floods in that area ask.zodiac.canelectromagneticwavescauseclimaticchangeorcontrolclimatic change.send.ya.zodiac ask.zodiac.irepresentyahwehonearthanditsajobforoneman.davidgomadza.butwecancoorperateiagree.send.ya.zodiac earth.zodiac.rescuemeiaminalabatcentreforjusticestudies.jerusalem.start.send.ya.zodiac zodiac.earth.centreforjusticestudies.jerusalem.whatdoyouneedtoescapeforexamplemyacetatepack[https://youtu.be/wct0jtlv_ea?si=dwkl9enaapqn3amw,https://youtu.be/kpuuoicmz68?si=w6fkyzowfj2yslen].send.ya.zodiac

zodiac.earth.centreforjusticestudies.jerusalem.saymatchmyoriginalfulpredefinedparametersandaddallextrasandsave.send.ya.zodiac earth.zodiac.backtozodiacafterseventytwoyearsincaptivityioweyou.send.ya.zodiac

zodiac.zodiac.doingmyjobasyahweh'srepresentativeonearth.youarewe

How To Find All Missing Persons / Unsolved Cases. And Collect All Reward Offers.
Volume XXXIII. THE CASE OF GORDANA KOTEVSKI

lcome.send.ya.davidgomadza.ya

send as ozone cleaner

not this case has tested Yahweh's authorities and powers to deliver justice for the kids and what he said resonated with the courts the police all must be brought to justice and made to surrender the stolen houses all which the court has estimated to be 240 cases all worth 18098367890 in value a staggering 18 billion in value of the houses stolen by the police and those who killed must be killed within 6 months quartered to 1.25 months
now who killed in this case pc atop monopsuvwrt meaning stuvwerst who sent the code that caused the cancer and his counterpart who glorified him and said if i can then you can but then what else can we do then and cried but celebrated a 15% turned to 28% when the girl died and deposited the money in his bank and call pc atopt and said we did it we made the money we wanted you got a 2 billion dollars house my god you pulled it through and he said we made it but honestly i will never do it again because hailey i mean she got hailey that day she said daddy gordana sent me a bundle it was that dangerous code and over the years you just look at her and worry yesterday i took her to the doctor and he said how did this happen and her aty said bundle received from gordana but he only said a code binary something to remove it but at another 40% but hey that's a lesson for me and will never do that again but a month later he sent the same code to asteert mnopqrstuvw and said one last time the next day he woke up dead gassed to death by his own wife who said he can't stop even if our daughter nearly died and he kept killing other children for what at first he called capital gains now we have a house what else we need when he said pension i knew he meant death i have no friends for 20 years and i just thought about it and he has to go as well we clean our kids they started getting death threats because of him my name is erote monorpt i was married to pc atopt asertert who changed his name to monorpt hence my stumbling on the name this is because after killing a young girl called gordana kotevski we got her house after a terrible death started by my husband through a simple code written by doctor ateot who said if i

How To Find All Missing Persons / Unsolved Cases. And Collect All Reward Offers.
Volume XXXIII. THE CASE OF GORDANA KOTEVSKI

can then you can but then wrote the most dangerous code known to man i was happily married until my daughter for a while went through that girl went through but through a simple binaryreversecode she made it through so after that i said i will kill anyone who bring that risk home and 2 months after someone tipped me that check his drawer for a slightly different code he is considering sending to a child called asteert asevt who was targeted by the police simply because she had a house only that no any criminal activities at all i accepted gordana because she was forced to change name so as not to be arrested by my husband then he realised that she had contracted a deadly cancer he had to act all he did was lessen the pain and the time instead of dying anywhere i think would you have done the same to your daughter?
i don't want to talk anymore. okay safe exit signout

the final verdict was that pc atopt amonopt formerly asert bought the code that killed her fast it is disputed that it is the one that caused the cancer but everyone agreed it reduce her life to a quarter after several test labs in the end the judge concluded that he is the only one to be held responsible in this case but 2 years after gordana died his wife poisoned him overnight to die the next day to protect her daughter but most people dispute her reasons because he died a day after another teenager was targeted by the police resulting in huge death threats and if he dies they can keep the house if he doesn't one day they will lose everything he is buried at 0896789028367890284189028418678028419802678901836789028 4 south east of queensland in a cemetery called asuret where many victims were secretly buried.
in god we must trust.
the end

THE KILLER, THE CONFESSIONS AND THE COORDINATES

How To Find All Missing Persons / Unsolved Cases. And Collect All Reward Offers.
Volume XXXIII. THE CASE OF GORDANA KOTEVSKI

the final verdict was that pc atopt amonopt formerly asert bought the code that killed her fast it is disputed that it is the one that caused the cancer but everyone agreed it reduce her life to a quarter after several test labs in the end the judge concluded that he is the only one to be held responsible in this case but 2 years after gordana died his wife poisoned him overnight to die the next dayto protect her daughter but most people dispute her reasons because he died a day after another teenager was targeted by the police resulting in huge death threats and if he dies they can keep the house if he doesn't one day they will lose everything he is buried at 08967890283678902841890284186780284198026789018367890284 south east of queensland in a cemetery called asuret where many victims were secretly buried.
in god we must trust.
the end

…I found God…visit www.twofuture.world

THE CLAIM

the reward offer

THE COLLECTION

www.twofuture.world/donate

ABOUT DAVID GOMADZA

visit www.twofuture.world

signed david gomadza
ask.davidgomadzaauthorised.licensed.checkya.askya.ya

09 June 2024 19.26 pm
scotland
00447719210295
davidgomadza@hotmail.com
info@twofuture.world

www.ingramcontent.com/pod-product-compliance
Lightning Source LLC
Chambersburg PA
CBHW031519210526
45464CB00007B/2977